# THE
# PRAYER
# D(OF)ONNY

*A Resolute Heart*

# SANDRA QUERIN

Paperback ISBN 978-1-960007-60-5
eBook ISBN 978-1-960007-61-2

Published by
**Orison Publishers, Inc.**
PO Box 188
Grantham, PA 17027
www.OrisonPublishers.com

# Table of Contents

# Foreword

*The Prayer of Donny* is a powerful new weapon against the battles of life. What a gift to those who face attacks! Here are secrets of victory forged in the intense heat of spiritual warfare, in the midst of incredible trial. Sandi's trials are beyond what she mentions in these pages. I know, because Mechelle and I witnessed her journey and the price she paid for these powerful truths as she imparted them into her dear son.

*Evangelist Mario Murillo*
*Mario Murillo Ministries*
*Lafayette, Tennessee, 2024*

# Preface

"Pain and trial do not cause you to be something new; they cause you to be who you really are. Since identity is found where you spend your time, be sure to spend your time well…. You will need a quality of time in your bones someday."

–Donny Querin

Life gets in the way of our progress sometimes. In fact, it gets in the way most of the time. It has taken me seventeen years to write this book and finish the "Honest to God" series, following *The Prayer of Job* and *The Prayer of Moses*.

I am elated to share with you the power of what comes this way. Each page came at a price for me, and I cannot help but think that the Lord had *you* on His mind throughout this journey of pain and redemption.

When grief comes to visit, in whatever form it comes, it brings with it a whirlwind that has the power to remain. There is no stopping the waves of grief; one can only lean upon the Lord to ride those waves.

When catastrophic grief nails you to a wall, it has a purpose. It wants to make you live in a grief-stricken state of horror and terror for the rest of your life. This does not have to be so! There is joy on the other side of understanding. Grief will last a lifetime, yes, but it is part of the glory of the Lord upon you. So, in all these things, you and I must walk and not crawl, whenever it is possible. Then, in time, we will find ourselves marching.

We can rejoice as we walk with Christ with grief as our companion, without ever being grief-stricken. All of what you have suffered and overcome is of great value; please don't discount it or run from it. Many people who suffer from grief don't recognize it as they try to manage their wounds of trauma, loss and disappointment.

This book is not solely "about grief," but when grief hits you the way it hit me…I am here to tell you that it lingers in everything we touch, not in bitterness or as a grudge, but as an honor. It is an honor to see the Almighty bend His gracious heart toward us in the depths of our deepest pain. The Bible says that God will rescue us out of all our trouble (Psalm 34:19). I have lived through enough to know this is true.

He, as I have found, never leaves us. We prevail as we walk across the prayers of the saints while Jesus holds our hand. As we remain in the character of Christ, our pain and trouble all become a blessing, and the chaos removes itself.

As we go on this journey of spiritual empowerment, leaving our graveclothes behind and walking out of the tomb with power, we will find our wounds giving way to design and purpose, and we become overcomers who walk in authority.

*Freedom* is a beautiful word, but *liberty* is better. Freedom gives us the permission to do a thing while liberty dictates that we take our authority to enforce it.

March away from the jail masters who have kept you in bondage and come with me as we walk across this fallen Eden to the glory of God with liberty and courage as our companions.

> [The Lord] *comforts us in all our troubles so that we can comfort others. When they are troubled, we will be able to give them the same comfort that God has given us* (2 Corinthians 1:4 NLT).

# Introduction

Alimping soldier does no good in a fight. Whatever you are suffering, these pages will teach you how to get well and then fight and force the enemy to suffer for the loss he caused, the damage he did, and the attempt he made to diminish the glory of God in your life. People say not to trust someone without a limp, but the opposite is true. A limp cured is a refusal to bow to any lingering wounds.

Leukemia came upon my boy and plowed a path of horror through my soul that would take almost four years to carve. It shouted, "Live in pain!" as it took my beloved son from me. But, in that moment, God shouted back, "We shall prevail through this pain!"

I have since realized that leukemia did not take my boy; rather, he was destined to go. He had a time to come and live and a time to return from whence he came. The hand of the Lord was gracefully—or as gracefully as I would allow it—in charge of all these things.

Standing on this side of that river of pain, forever stained and marked from my journey to this point, I have learned that writing this book required me to cling to the cross of Christ in a way that I never had before.

Tragedy and disaster give unique and beautiful color to the canvas of our lives. The Lord allows these things to be part of us so that we have new and original ways to glorify and honor Him in our pain. He does not require it, but our lives do. Our lives crave to glorify the Lord. From the moment we are born, there is a yearning and desire in us to glorify God. Somehow, when we grow older, we often forget that principle. We forget what that desire looks like. We forget to remember God.

*And we know that God causes everything to work together for the good of those who love God and are called according to his purpose for them. ... What shall we say about such wonderful things as these? If God is for us, who can ever be against us? Since he did not spare even his own Son but gave him up for us all, won't he also give us everything else?* (Romans 8:28,31–32 NLT)

I shall endeavor to share visions, dreams and inspiration through the pages of this book, with the Word of God leading the way. "Waiting on God" seems to be a lost form of art, and that is something we will address. Read the chapter titles in the Contents, and you will find yourself getting excited for the amazing journey we will take as, grief-stricken victims no more, we walk in a powerful portion of our Godly authority over our grief.

My son Donny knew that he had to remain whole through his trial to fully honor God, and he will teach us how here. "If you trust Jesus, things will be okay. If you don't trust Him, nothing will ever be okay. My pain will not force me to dishonor God," is something he said only a few months before he passed away.

Donny was gentle in manner and resolute in execution. He could make a room notice God in him. He demonstrated what it looks like when a man carries God around. His life became a parable of God's grace and courage, so beautiful was Christ in him.

I waited thirty-three years for God to heal me of cystic fibrosis and eight years (just recently) for Him to heal me of systemic mastocytosis and its complications. All the longsuffering healings and instant miracles along the way are too many to count or recall.

However, the question lingers for many: "Why doesn't God just fix everything now?" Certainly, it would appear to be a more efficient form of time management, to say the least. But the ways of God are known and unknown to us, all at the same time. What I do know is this: Leave it be. Let God be God.

Grief shouted, "Live in pain!" as it took my beloved Donny from me. But, in that moment, as I said before, God shouted back, "We shall prevail through this pain!" Everyone deals with grief differently. I lost a piece of my soul when my boy left. My daughter was punched in the face, knowing that her "Irish twin" would be no more. One of the hardest pieces of this loss was to watch my lovely daughter Cynthia collapse into her own soul as she waited for redemption of a pain that would never come, for her brother was gone.

His wife, my daughter-in-law, was forced into widowhood as a young woman with her teacher, friend and husband not there to love her through life. His father would grieve the loss of his surname upon the earth. Aunts, uncles, cousins, grandparents, friends and every person my Donny ever met still grieve at his going, even these fourteen years later. But this I know: God is perfect, and we must prevail as we yield to His will.

Loss—any loss or disappointment—can rip at the fibers of our being as if to dare us to not go on. Somehow, it is able to compel us to recoil and become average. Pain and suffering by design, for saints, should provoke us to Godliness because, when we are found in Christ and He in us, we must go on. We go on because we have this Anchor of our soul (Hebrews 6:19).

The dynamic power of being bought by the blood of Jesus draws a circle around us and shouts to the enemy, "You cannot pass this way." But we must stand and not relent; we must stand and not give in to the temptation of being found lukewarm in the presence of God.

We are not stricken, so we hold nothing higher than the bloodline of Jesus Christ; rather, we forge ahead and soldier on, not afraid of feeling our grief, not terrified of pain or suffering, so that we may lay those things down at the foot of the cross.

We who have suffered loss have a ditch in our souls, a beautiful scar—one that will always be there. We can choose to allow the Lord to plant fragrant flowers in that ditch, or we can let it remain as a mud pit that will forever attempt to bury us. We must carry our cross and climb our hill before we lay these burdens down at the empty tomb, where we will be resurrected from this pain and trial. I adjure you, don't settle for mud!

People tell me—and perhaps they have told you—to "move on" or "get over" it. Ah, but they don't understand. I shall never "move on" from or "get over" my son. I will forever have this ditch in my soul. I will forever have a loss. However, I am able, as I hold nothing higher than the bloodline of Jesus Christ in my life, to allow the Holy Spirit to plant flowers in that ditch. We all have ditches in our souls; some are beautiful and some are not. Some smell of a sweet fragrance while some have a lingering stench. Some have been handed over to the Almighty, and some have not.

Here in these pages, you will learn how to be an overcoming conqueror. Come with me as we walk through the making of a man, his mission and the misery that would give way to majesty. It is my extreme pleasure to take you with me through *The Prayer of Donny*.

## CHAPTER ONE

# Christic in Me, the Hope of Glory!

> "Until we are willing to learn *who* Jesus is, we will not be able to have *what* He is. We must walk in who Jesus is if we are to abide in Him and operate in the fruit of the Spirit. We only begin to be who we are destined to be when we cease to whine and blame others and begin to search for God's love, ideals and justice, which should regulate our lives."
>
> –Donny Querin

This book does not intend to be about Donny more than it intends to be lessons learned by Donny. However, to get the one, we must pass through the other. So, to that end, I give you my son.

*Donald Angelo Querin.* He came like a bullet with his hands clenched in fists upon his tiny baby chest at his birth on March 13, 1981. Thirteen hours of hard labor were my portion, and his life would be one that would repeat that sentiment over and over again, as he was an incredibly difficult joy!

I think he knew more than most people from the minute he could speak, so he was in a seemingly continual state of frustration for many years. It would take me a decade to catch up with him, if I ever really did. I am not sure.

From the earliest time of his childhood that I can remember, I hear him asking me, "Mama, what makes a great man?" I would tell him, "Wisdom and kindness." When he asked how to get them, I told him to learn of Jesus because He was the wisest and the kindest. I also told him to read what Solomon wrote. So, his quest began, along with all the difficulties of childhood that everyone encounters. But he had a strong start.

Donny decided very young (I think at birth) that he was too cool for sleep. Two or three hours of sleep per night and one twenty-minute nap were all he would tolerate. I often slept on the floor outside his room so I would know if he got up or not. He unplugged any monitoring device we had at the time. I didn't want to put a lock on the outside of his door because I didn't want him to have a terrible memory of being trapped somewhere.

When he was eleven months old, I gave birth to his sister Cynthia. You never saw a child so happy as he was. In his thirst for adventure, when Cynthia could walk at eleven months old, he found many grand mishaps to be part of and took her along. She adored him and willingly embraced each escapade.

When they were one and two years old, he liked to sneak into her room and get her out of her crib in the middle of the night, kick out the screen at the window, and go "on an adventure" up and down the street, playing with toys that were left in other children's yards.

More times than I can remember, I would find a note taped to my car window or front door or a phone message, stating, "I have the children; you take a nap!" Most people knew I had cystic fibrosis and that its complications kept me ill from time to time, and no sleep didn't help anything. (It would take over thirty years, but the Lord came with force to heal me one glorious day.)

I had to wrap a chain with a lock around the refrigerator because Donny would open it, push some chairs over, and unload the entire freezer and refrigerator into the heater vents. He would add his stuffed toys to the pile of milk and eggs and say that his "animals are going on an adventure." You haven't lived until you have smelled that mess!

Once I came running down the hall at 3:00 a.m. to his yell of, "Help, Mama, help." He could not have been more than two years old. He had climbed up on chairs that he stacked and was hanging from the top of the freezer, which was chained shut. The chairs had fallen, and he didn't have a way to get down. He was the strongest child I had ever met. I lowered him down from there, and I thought the horror on his face would stop the adventures, but it did not. He would come up with one idea, and we would solve that problem; then he would come up with another idea. We were always one step behind his genius.

"Christ in me, the hope of glory" looked different on Donny than it did on anyone else! During those early years, I would just pray that we could all survive how awesome he was. When he was being incredibly difficult, I would look at him and say, "You are just too awesome, son, just too awesome."

A spanking didn't faze him; a "time out" was laughable. He seemed to enjoy the challenge of it all with his joyful, happy, tender heart. Once he was running out to the back of the yard to climb over the neighbor's barbed wire fence to play with the cows in a field by the little creek in the Sonoma Valley where we lived. I told him that if he got through that fence, he was going to get a spanking. (He often did, for he loved those cows. The cuts on his hands from the barbed wire fence he shimmied through, he wore like a badge.)

He was barely two-and-a-half years old, and he just told me to "go get the spoon" because he was doing it! My husband and I ended up building a fence with one-by-six boards spaced vertically so Donny couldn't climb them. We stacked all his toys on top of each other and then added four more feet in height to the fence to trap him, and it worked—until it didn't.

My husband was gone almost all the time building houses all over California and Nevada, so he wasn't there to help. Many friends and family members were nearby, but somebody cannot spend the night every night to help you manage your ninja child. When it got completely unbearable, I would just sit and weep.

Once, during a time like this, Donny walked up to me and quoted a scripture he learned in junior church under my sister Gail's direction. He held my hand and said, "Don't worry, Mama. Jeremiah 33:3 says that God will show you great and mighty things that you don't even know about yet" (NKJV). He was five years old. I knew I was in for it from that moment on as he proceeded to dig up a young cherry tree out back with his baby sister to see if he could! He could. I was tired.

Listen, I was a very attentive mother, but you'd never know it with these crazy stories. It only took him twenty seconds to spin the world off its axis. Twenty seconds!

From the time he could read, he became a student of the proverbs of Solomon. He could just about quote the entire book of Proverbs by the time he was twenty. However, these proverbs did not start in his head. They ruminated and simmered in his soul and made their way to his heart, and then the mind remembered as it was transformed. *Knowing scripture isn't the thing. Living it is.*

Inspired statements formed in his mind, making him the most quotable boy I ever knew. I am grateful that I wrote down so many of his thoughts. The greatest thing he would learn is that Jesus is in us, trying to be seen by the world. In the end, the world would marvel at Donny's great faith and lack of fear; getting him there, though, would prove to be a challenge on every single level. *Most worthwhile quests start out as great trials before they give way to triumph.*

While possessing his learner's permit in preparation for his driver's license, we were running errands in a large town he had never driven in before. He began to turn onto a one-way street, heading the wrong way. All the cars were stopped at a stop light down at the other end, so it did not register to him that this was a one-way street. I asked him if he knew what he was doing, and he said, "Yes." So I said, "Okay, then."

As he pulled out into four lanes of cars coming at him (for the light had just turned), he ended up on the side of the road having barely avoided an accident. I was laughing, and he shouted that it wasn't funny. I said to him, "Don't say you know what you are doing, if you don't know what you are doing." He began to *seek to understand rather than be understood* after that.

After receiving his driver's license, he and his old '64 Chevy truck would get busy laying rubber all over town. He never swore or drank, but that truck…. He loved to drive it fast, so he did. He was, by his own admission, resolute in nature, so getting an idea out of his head once it got in there was a task. He didn't understand, if the behavior wasn't hurting anyone, why it was bad. The police would have a different view. The discipline of life was beginning to bear down upon him.

One evening, a police officer came to my door and handed me Donny's keys and Donny. He said that Donny and his friends were tearing up the road all over town, and the police expected me to put a stop to it and handle my boy. A friend was over, and after the police left, she said, "Oh, that's nothing. He is just sowing some innocent wild oats." I yelled and said, "I am not raising a bowl of oatmeal! I am raising a man." Donny lost his license for a month. But that wouldn't stop him and his truck, "Rosie," from getting into many more "fun adventures," which would commence in exactly thirty-two days!

He told me that it was a dumb law, so he shouldn't have to follow it. I let him know that until he changed the law, he would have to abide by it. That is part of Christ dwelling in us. That is part of the world being able to see Him in us. If our fleshly desires are hiding Jesus from view, then He cannot be the hope of the world to the people. Donny would master discipline, but it would take time.

*He was blessed with bravery and the courage to walk out what bravery would allow him to consider.* Keeping those superpowers anchored to the cross of Christ would be the quest of his life and serve him well, but while he was a baby boy...he was a baby boy!

> *...And this is the secret: Christ lives in you. This gives you assurance of sharing his glory* (Colossians 1:27 NLT).

> *To whom God would make known what is the riches of the glory of this mystery among the Gentiles; which is Christ in you, the hope of glory* (Colossians 1:27 KJV).

If the world can see Jesus instead of us—if we are hiding behind Him and allowing Him to shine and do the heavy lifting—then the world would know Him. However, so often we step ahead of Christ. Then the world sees us long before they see Him and, thereby, rarely ever see Christ in us.

If our flesh is laid low enough, then we will find ourselves hiding behind Christ in safety, tucked into the cleft of the rock. What prevents people from seeing Christ in us is *us*! Only as we cast our flesh and its wicked desires down is Jesus lifted up.

Here is why: We are too consumed with being somebody in Christ. You see, we have it backwards. *The theme of life is not who I am in Christ, but rather who He is in me.* We have to allow that switch. Jesus won't fight us for position in our lives; we have to freely give it to Him and not take it back.

When trials come (and they will), we are not going to have time to get awesome so we can stand through the trial; we are going to have to already be on the spot. Sure, trials grow us and we all become better through trials and the affliction of life; Jesus did. But if we are so far off the mark when the trial comes that we have to scramble to make it, then we will miss the beauty and the opportunity of the trial and our deliverance from it will be frustrated and delayed. You see, God cares far more for us than what we can do for Him; this is eternal truth. We matter to Him, but we need to take the time to *know* Him. His ways are beyond His acts (Psalm 103:7).

When flesh becomes king in our lives, then when the true king comes to our house, we don't recognize Him. The flesh must be forced low so that Christ can be seen more than our flesh can. We cannot lift Jesus up if our arms are full of ourselves. Christ will not dwell in us richly and the world will not see the hope of glory if there is more of us than of Him. Carnal Christianity seems to be a race to see who is "in Christ" to a greater degree, when *Christ* wants to be *in us*. One has an opinion while the other does not.

So, how is "Christ in you" accomplished? You must decide that it is what you want. If you have a made-up mind, then the fight is over. *What you believe determines how you behave, and how you behave determines the outcome.* The outcome will usually confirm or deny what you believe, even if it is wrong. The self-sabotage of life occurs because you believe wrong. Change the belief and the behavior changes, and thereupon the outcome changes. Consequences are minimized and Christ is seen in you as glorious.

I often hear, after individuals have been led astray either by themselves or others, "See, I am just a loser, just like always." They confirm their negative self upon themselves, and the cycle continues. *Belief becomes the foundation of what will happen to us.* These thoughts and actions, based on a false identity, steer our lives, and the struggle continues.

If I am to believe that Christ is in me and that He is the hope of glory to the whole world, then there is no room left to believe anything else. My thoughts of inadequacy should buckle under the weight of this great revelation. There is no room for both thoughts. Rejection, abandonment, guilt or shame cannot live under the mighty declaration of "Christ lives in me." When my identity is anchored in Christ, it creates a "spiritual giant" of who I will become *in Him.*

Donny had a hard time in high school. He would not study, and he did not want to go to school because the school was trying to survive a crisis of a lack of teachers. He could not wrap his mind around the fact that a music teacher was trying to teach him math and doing it wrong. He could not understand why the English teacher could not spell (she was a P.E. teacher, evidently). He wanted no part of it, and I could not make him tolerate it after I caught huge and obvious errors in the homework they graded. The school defended its position, so we were out. (Cynthia seemed to be flexible enough to weather this educational storm, but not this one!)

After a two-year battle, I pulled him out of high school as a junior, and he passed the California Proficiency Exam in the top ten percent of the state. He went to work at sixteen years old, and at eighteen was in Teen Mania Ministries. There he stayed for four years, attended college, met his future bride, and accomplished amazing things around the world. Later he earned his degree in Organizational Management and Psychology along with becoming a certified personal trainer.

Donny was on the edge of believing he was "one who could not finish a task," and his life started to show signs of that belief. When he was removed from the situation that had put a "burr under his saddle," he thrived and leaned forward to reach his goals. I told him, "I guess you are just too awesome for this school; let's find another way." And, we did.

When your belief system starts to slide from awesome to unawesome, please remove the obstacle or situation that is creating the chaos and set yourself free. God so often helps out in unsuspecting and even mysterious ways, but you have to be paying attention and grasp the "unction" and peace of the situation.

That is not to say, if any little thing is adverse, to remove it. No! Those adversities build us. It is through trials that we learn to fight for the triumphs. It is through great sorrow that we push harder than ever before to find our joy. It is through affliction that we learn to seek truth and trust. Through great price comes great power. We are not just simply saved from this or into that. *We are redeemed.* "Behaving redeemed" must always be considered.

Redemption means that you do not forget the Lord; it means you recognize that you have been *bought* with an incredibly high price. To know the power of redemption means that you do not, because you cannot, act out as a vessel with your own opinion. Because you are owned, you naturally defer to the One who paid for your freedom. It is the difference between being called and being chosen. One is invited; the other accepts the invitation. (See Matthew 22:14.) Herein lies the difference between being a "vessel for honor" or a vessel "for dishonor" in the house of God (2 Timothy 2:20–21 NKJV).

There are those unsurmountable situations that come to clip our souls, and those situations we should remove from our path. Things that God does not deem worthy are things that should be removed. When something does not force you to grow, force it away from yourself. *What causes you to disobey should go away!*

Many people stay in dead-end jobs, entirely unfilled, because they think that they "have to," and long after the Lord leaves the building, they remain. When a trial has outlived its usefulness, it simply causes damage. Pay attention to where the peace of God is dwelling in your life and follow it. His peace can remain in a situation that you hate. His peace can be absent in a situation you love. In the beautiful name of Jesus, you must know the difference. Pray. If you have peace, pursue. If there is no peace, there should be no pursuit (see Colossians 3:15).

Peace is Jesus sleeping in the back of the boat. Don't let the storm get in you; you get in the storm. You do that by understanding that you are held within the arms of the Master of the storm—even when your chaos and trials were caused by your own hand. Sin usually comes from self-imposed situations. Then guilt overtakes us. That's the oldest trick in the book; don't fall for it.

*This is the specialty of Christ: loving us through our manmade madness.*

I used to teach an Ethics, Law and Business classes at several different universities in California before I started to travel and preach full-time. Donny loved to attend the classes from time to time, and it was the funniest thing to have your fourteen-year-old child want to watch you teach a college class. Among other things, in an ethics class, you learn fundamental questions to ask yourself when you approach a challenge in life or an ethical dilemma. Three of them are listed here:

1. Would you tell a child to do this?
2. Would you be happy if what you are doing was spread across the news and social media with the guarantee that everyone you know would hear about or read it?
3. Would you want this done to you?

If any of the answers are "no," then you must not perform the act or get involved in the situation. You will discover that peace is not hard to find if you stop, think and ponder for just a moment or two. The price is usually your flesh, so don't give the spoiled brat its way. Hold strong and fast in the faith by which you are saved (1 Corinthians 15:2).

I have used this technique for many years. When the flesh rises up and we refuse to hear the Lord because our fleshly desires are trying to force an emotional decision, our free will begins to tilt. When this happens, we try to become more spiritual than we were a few minutes earlier, but often it is too late; our soul, body and mind have joined forces against our spirit by then. So, we need to have tools and weapons to combat the flesh. Some are spiritual and some are very practical. Redeemed people will run to the cure and embrace it because they understand the price.

If you only believe you are walking in the salvation of Christ and you have this gift, then, in time, you will stop protecting that gift and let your opinions and wants cover it. Redeemed people protect their salvation because they are aware of the cost. *Donny knew this, to his pain, as he carried his heavy cross up a steep hill.*

To phrase it another way, don't do something that you will regret later. Don't do something that will make a bad memory out of the moment. Those moments cannot be rewritten, and they will bless you or curse you by your own hand. Remember that you are redeemed and that Christ lives in you. Don't drag Him off to do stupid stuff.

At every hospital we went to in the course of Donny's illness, people would find Christ. They would say they could feel a supernatural power in Donny. Before we would go to the hospital, we would pray, and Donny would always say, "Let's go fishing, Ma." We did. When Christ is in you and you allow Him to shine as the hope of glory, people notice it, because most people are looking for hope.

A surrendered vessel falls into the Lord while a yielded vessel falls into the Lord and doesn't care about the surrounding conditions. A yielded vessel prays, "Lord, I didn't get what I wanted last time we went down this road, and it messed me up pretty badly. But here I am, and I trust You to do what You say is right. I am giving in to the process. I will not judge You or fight You about the outcome. I just want You and what You want. In fact, if You want to allow that rotten thing to happen again, I am up for it because I know that You go with me." Trust is learned there.

When Leukemia struck Donny at twenty-five years old, he would learn to live that prayer, not just believe it.

> "The person who does not see the need to rise up to a challenge is one who has underestimated God and overestimated himself! Compassion without action is equal to the deepest hatred."
>
> –Donny Querin

## CHAPTER TWO

# Dominion and Authority

"If we are not willing to be corrected, we walk in darkness. Jesus knew His purpose, and He didn't let the human emotions that swarmed about Him in the Garden confuse Him. We allow God to cultivate His love in our lives by the way we are willing to live our lives. Authority is found in our identity, and identity is gained where we spend time."
                                                                    –Donny Querin

When Donny became ill with leukemia at twenty-five years old, we looked at each other together, alone in the doctor's office, and said, "Okay, yeah, we can do leukemia." Time would test our brave statement over the next four years.

Here is this gladiator of a man, a beast with four percent body fat, only sick briefly twice in his life, staring down the barrel of a killer. So, we marched. We all did. His bride-to-be stopped her life to embrace his. His little Irish twin, Cynthia, raced over from the coast, and the bedside vigils began.

There was Donny, admitted to the hospital with his spleen swollen into just about every other organ. He could not breathe. He was vomiting.

We were trying to ask the right questions, but we had never gone this way before. We did not know what to ask or what to do, save this one thing: we could pray. We could lean on Jesus. We could trust Him. So, we did.

Donny would march up and down the hospital hallways kicking his IV pole along as he went, with fifty-pound barbells in each hand. He pumped iron as he went, as if to shout in the face of leukemia, "You cannot walk this road with me!"

As he marched, blood would spray out of his nose. He didn't care. I finally put a face mask on him to catch the blood. He would march until he would drop.

I would usually catch him just in time, as I followed him with a wheelchair. He despised it, but he found himself grateful for it, as the floor was a liability. He had already chipped a tooth from treating his stubbornness as faith.

Three weeks had him in remission. He got out of the hospital just in time for his sister's wedding.

Three months later, he would get a blood transfusion on the morning of his own wedding. Afterwards, he enjoyed a California honeymoon with the great love of his life, sweet Amy.

Today people want to shout their problems out and command God to do something about it. They call it authority when really it is fear.

Faith is not a seasoning you sprinkle on a situation; rather, it is a tangible element that rises up from within a situation that must be dealt with. Some will deal; some will not.

Some will notice what is going on and appropriate their trust in Christ to deal with it; others will just stand there and shout about what needs to be done. When you operate out of friendship and fellowship with Jesus, you are okay with whatever direction He wants to go because you trust Him. Real authority in Christ is found in your identity in Him, which comes from fellowship with Him.

The enemy of your soul has no place in the kingdom of God and should be dealt with aggressively, but to command God...well, that is the practice of fools. I feel that grace has been greatly misunderstood, but that is a story for another time.

Six months later, the villain returned.

Donny began to ask, "Why?" I remember telling him that we don't ask why; we *live* the why. We *are* the why. Christ *is* the why. Trust connects those two things.

He had to get to the place where it didn't matter where he ended up, just that Jesus was going with him. But, getting there would take some doing because he thought, perhaps, he could punch his way out of this ring.

He wondered, "Did I cut my hair like Samson? Why is this happening to me?" These are questions that he would ask as he was curled up on the floor in agony, vomiting, struggling to breathe, as an unfair saga unfolded upon him.

At one point, the vomiting and shaking were so bad that the doctors became concerned. There was no reason for it. His fingertips were all infected and "blown out."

On top of all that, he had something called mucositis from the tip of his tongue all the way to the end of his intestines. He was in incredible pain, and they couldn't get it managed. He started to get depressed and shouted, "Ma, I can't take it anymore. I can't. I am on the edge."

That was not a statement that I wanted to hear from my warrior son, so I shouted back, "If someone is pushing you to the edge of a cliff, you have two options. Either turn around and push him back, or fall off the cliff. You have to remember who you are and that Christ is in you. These are not negotiable. If the enemy is bringing distress and depression on you, then kick him out and go through this trial clean and ready, or give up. Decide who you are."

I left the room and wished I could have slammed the hospital door, but those doors don't slam. I sat outside the room and listened. He was weeping, and it almost killed me not to go to my son.

But, he was a man, and this was man's work. He would have to decide who he was. He would have to remember. I would not handicap his faith by intervening. That was hard, truly hard.

His tears stopped, and then the lion roared. I began to cry very loud tears as he shouted at the enemy, commanding him to get off of him. My boy made it back.

He was throwing things around and yelling at the enemy of his soul and stating his authority in Christ over all things and that he would only yield to the efforts of God in him.

Then he said, "Devil, you will not force me to blaspheme God by bringing trouble within my trial. I will believe and I will hope, no matter what, and you cannot force me to become a vessel of dishonor. I refuse depression and anxiety. I will allow Christ to occupy here." I will never forget Donny's words. That was an hour of joy.

I am here to tell you that the boy was only depressed once again for a few hours in almost four years of illness because of the pain and because he "missed his life."

Still, he quickly remembered to ask for prayer and to take a stand against what was afflicting him. Authority comes from where we spend our time; it is either part of our identity or it is not. It cannot be borrowed; it has to be owned. Owning it costs. Some will pay; some will not.

Donny was in the Word of God, and it was in him. So, although it was hard—very hard—he sailed right on through.

> [May] *the eyes of your understanding being enlightened; that ye may know what is the hope of his calling, and what the riches of the glory of his inheritance in the saints, and what is the exceeding greatness of his power to us-ward who believe, according to the working of his mighty power, which he wrought in Christ, when he raised him from the dead, and set him at his own right hand in the heavenly places, far above all principality, and power, and might, and dominion, and every name that is named, not only in this world, but also in that which is to come: and hath put all things under his feet, and gave him to be the head over all things to the church, which is his body, the fulness of him that filleth all in all* (Ephesians 1:18–23 KJV).

Our authority in Christ will decide if we will fail or succeed. God gave man dominion over the earth. Man gave it to Satan. Jesus came to give us back dominion through the authority of His shed blood and resurrected body.

We were given dominion and authority. But, after the fall, after Noah and his lovely ark, we find that we no longer "had" dominion; we would have to take it. Jesus made the way for that to happen.

Having power in a situation happens only as you take your authority within it. When you do that, you have dominion in it. Then you control not the outcome, but what affects you *during the process* of the outcome. *Therein lies true and mature faith; it trusts, and it will wait.*

If the Holy Spirit says, "This or that will be," then it will be if you believe it. But, if you have not been given such a statement, there is no sense in you pushing your weight around, only to experience a failure that makes God look bad.

In a ball game, many pieces are needed to make it work. Think of the players and referees for a moment. Suppose one player dominates the game. Undeniably, this player is the best. He is big and strong with talent that has been kissed by skill. He has dominion.

However, the referee has authority over the one who dominates. The referee may be small and frail and no match for the ball player in a real fight but oddly has the power to eliminate any player he would choose.

Authority surpasses dominion every time. Coming in Christ's authority obliterates any evil force that has taken dominion over your life. We are told to take dominion and authority. You figure that out.

Faith cannot be fabricated. It either is, or it is not. But at all times, we trust. Trust is mature faith; it has eliminated the human element with all of its fears, decrees, silly proclamations, declarations and opinions.

If the unction doesn't rise up within you, then it is not there, and God has another purpose or path. The key is to trust Jesus, walk with Him, trust Him and, when the enemy attacks, rebuke him and take your position behind Christ, hiding in the safety of His protection.

> *Submit yourselves therefore to God. Resist the devil, and he will flee from you* (James 4:7 KJV).

There is a submission that runs into a sort of perfection: it is to *yield*. If we cannot yield to God's will in the middle of our submission, then we will try to control the submission and wink at the obedience that it takes. Yielding does not care what God will do; it only wants to go with Him. Yielding will say, "This didn't work out so good last time, but I trust You to do what You want, even that thing I hate. Have at it, God. Be the Almighty!"

"It is not as important to measure whether we are slave or free, as it is to ask if we are free 'from' or free 'to.' The greatest irony and tragedy in life is our slavery to that which we fear. By refusing to risk failure, we refuse possible success and have therefore failed. Because preconception owns perception, we must always be ready for what God is calling us to do, beyond our abilities, limitations and desires. Don't get hung up on your destiny; identity is where it's at. Identity is found where time is spent. Authority is gained where identity is found. You may say you are seeking after Jesus, but the truth is this: *Your pursuit will always prove your desire.*"

–Donny Querin

## CHAPTER THREE

# *Hiding Behind Jesus*

"Prepare for God's will through obedience and submission to Christ in the fruit of the Spirit! The fact that it has been designed by God especially for us, just as each blessing and trial has been, should excite us past what it looks like or when it gets here.

"Preparation proves that we trust God to do what's best, and we are doing our best to be ready for whatever will come. We have to get good at preparing our hearts to accept His will and walk in His ways. Living a life that shouts 'Jesus is all that really matters' is the foundation of life. I have found this truth to be of great value as I wait on Him and His will, beyond a hope."

–Donny Querin

D onny was incredibly resolute in his faith, and if you asked him about himself, that is what he would say. Resolute in faith. Tender of heart. In all humility, he was very sure of some things.

One day while he was in high school here in the Central Valley of California, something happened that hurt his feelings. He was brokenhearted. I asked him why it hurt, and we talked about it. He was misunderstood and blamed for things he did not do.

It is quite a horrible thing to be so misunderstood and blamed. I reminded him, "They have misunderstood Christ in you and are blaming the Lord. They don't know it, but that is what they are doing, and Jesus will defend you."

The pain of Christ over these things is incredible. We asked Jesus to forgive them and began to consider the pain of the Lord in it, and, all of a sudden, Donny started "feeling sorry" for Jesus for having to take all of that upon Himself. He didn't feel bad for himself anymore but instead felt bad for Jesus, and he began to worship his Lord. From that day on, his worship changed him, just as it did Gideon in Judges 7:15–22.

When life comes at you like a bulldozer and there is nowhere to hide, hide behind Jesus! In fact, stay there. Be there all the time. If we stand behind Jesus when the darts are flying, then they will hit Him instead and we will spend our days being thankful to the Lord for "taking the hit" instead of being mad and unforgiving at the one who threw the fiery dart.

When we stay behind the Lord, it all becomes His problem, and we should mind our own business. Ephesians 6:16 (KJV) tells us to take "the shield of faith, wherewith ye shall be able to quench all the fiery darts of the wicked." Christ *is* that shield. But know that we are not instructed to only take one element of the armor; instead, we are told very clearly to take up the whole (full) armor of God (Ephesians 6:11).

As the darts fly, I find myself feeling bad for my Friend, Jesus, that He has to take so much pain for me. I know that He must have a broken heart over what was just said or done. Then He reminds me that He handled it all on Calvary (John 16:33).

Jesus not only died for our sins, for our right and privilege to know the Father, but He also is continually living out the benefit of the cross over our lives and taking everything that could happen to us from the cross to eternity. He bears it all on His shoulders today, just as He did so long ago on Calvary.

The only trouble is, we forget to stay behind Him for shelter in those situations. He is the shelter in the storm, the high tower and refuge. Only a fool walks out in front of the shield on a battleground.

You believe in Christ, and He is the shield of faith, so let Him be that for you. Jesus is brave enough and strong enough to handle you and your trouble.

> *He that dwelleth in the secret place of the most High shall abide under the shadow of the Almighty. I will say of the Lord, He is my refuge and my fortress: my God; in him will I trust. Surely he shall deliver thee from the snare of the fowler, and from the noisome pestilence. He shall cover thee with his feathers, and under his wings shalt thou trust: his truth shall be thy shield and buckler. Thou shalt not be afraid for the terror by night; nor for the arrow that flieth by day; nor for the pestilence that walketh in darkness; nor for the destruction that wasteth at noonday. A thousand shall fall at thy side, and ten thousand at thy right hand; but it shall not come nigh thee. Only with thine eyes shalt thou behold and see the reward of the wicked. Because thou hast made the Lord, which is my refuge, even the most High, thy habitation; there shall no evil befall thee, neither shall any plague come nigh thy dwelling. For he shall give his angels charge over thee, to keep thee in all thy ways. They shall bear thee up in their hands, lest thou dash thy foot against a stone. Thou shalt tread upon the lion and adder: the young lion and the dragon shalt thou trample under feet. Because he hath set his love upon me, therefore will I deliver him: I will set him on high, because he hath known my name. He shall call upon me, and I will answer him: I will be with him in trouble; I will deliver him, and honor him. With long life will I satisfy him, and shew him my salvation* (Psalm 91 KJV).

I would like to share a story here that I shared with Donny and Cynthia when they were quite young. Even if you are not quite young, I believe it will minister to you.

19

"The Ragman"[1]

I saw a strange sight. I stumbled upon a story most strange, like nothing my life, my street sense, my sly tongue had ever prepared me for.

Hush, child. Hush, now, and I will tell it to you.

Even before the dawn one Friday morning I noticed a young man, handsome and strong, walking the alleys of our City. He was pulling an old cart filled with clothes both bright and new, and he was calling in a clear tenor voice: "Rags!" Ah, the air was foul and the first light filthy to be crossed by such sweet music.

"Rags! New rags for old! I take your tired rags! Rags!"

"Now this is a wonder," I thought to myself, for the man stood six-feet-four, and his arms were like tree limbs, hard and muscular, and his eyes flashed intelligence. Could he find no better job than this, to be a ragman in the inner city?

I followed him. My curiosity drove me. And I wasn't disappointed.

Soon the Ragman saw a woman sitting on her back porch. She was sobbing into a handkerchief, sighing, and shedding a thousand tears. Her knees and elbows made a sad X. Her shoulders shook. Her heart was breaking.

The Ragman stopped his cart. Quietly, he walked to the woman, stepping round tin cans, dead toys, and Pampers.

"Give me your rag," he said so gently, "and I'll give you another."

He slipped the handkerchief from her eyes. She looked up, and he laid across her palm a linen cloth so clean and new that it shined. She blinked from the gift to the giver.

Then, as he began to pull his cart again, the Ragman did a strange thing: he put her stained handkerchief to his own face; and then *he* began to weep, to sob as

---

1 "Ragman" from Ragman: And Other Cries of Faith, Revised and Updated by Walter Wangerin Jr. Copyright (c) 2004 by Walter Wangerin Jr. Used by permission of HarperCollins Publishers.

grievously as she had done, his shoulders shaking. Yet she was left without a tear.

"This *is* a wonder," I breathed to myself, and I followed the sobbing Ragman like a child who cannot turn away from mystery.

"Rags! Rags! New rags for old!"

In a little while, when the sky showed grey behind the rooftops and I could see the shredded curtains hanging out black windows, the Ragman came upon a girl whose head was wrapped in a bandage, whose eyes were empty. Blood soaked her bandage. A single line of blood ran down her cheek.

Now the tall Ragman looked upon this child with pity, and he drew a lovely yellow bonnet from his cart.

"Give me your rag," he said, tracing his own line on her cheek, "and I'll give you mine."

The child could only gaze at him while he loosened the bandage, removed it, and tied it to his own head. The bonnet he set on hers. And I gasped at what I saw: for with the bandage went the wound! Against his brow it ran a darker, more substantial blood—his own!

"Rags! Rags! I take old rags!" cried the sobbing, bleeding, strong, intelligent Ragman.

The sun hurt both the sky, now, and my eyes; the Ragman seemed more and more to hurry.

"Are you going to work?" he asked a man who leaned against a telephone pole. The man shook his head.

The Ragman pressed him: "Do you have a job?"

"Are you crazy?" sneered the other. He pulled away from the pole, revealing the right sleeve of his jacket—flat, the cuff stuffed into the pocket. He had no arm.

"So," said the Ragman. "Give me your jacket, and I'll give you mine."

So much quiet authority in his voice!

The one-armed man took off his jacket. So did the Ragman—and I trembled at what I saw: for the Ragman's arm stayed in its sleeve, and when the other put it on he had two good arms, thick as tree limbs; but the Ragman had only one.

"Go to work," he said.

After that he found a drunk, lying unconscious beneath an army blanket, an old man, hunched, wizened, and sick. He took that blanket and wrapped it round himself, but for the drunk he left new clothes.

And now I had to run to keep up with the Ragman. Though he was weeping uncontrollably, and bleeding freely at the forehead, pulling his cart with one arm, stumbling for drunkenness, falling again and again, exhausted, old, old, and sick, yet he went with terrible speed. On spider's legs he skittered through the alleys of the City, this mile and the next, until he came to its limits, and then he rushed beyond.

I wept to see the change in this man. I hurt to see his sorrow. And yet I needed to see where he was going in such haste, perhaps to know what drove him so.

The little old Ragman—he came to a landfill. He came to the garbage pits. And then I wanted to help him in what he did, but I hung back, hiding. He climbed a hill. With tormented labor he cleared a little space on that hill. Then he signed. He lay down. He pillowed his head on a handkerchief and a jacket. He covered his bones with an army blanket. And he died.

Oh, how I cried to witness that death! I slumped in a junked car and wailed and mourned as one who has no hope—because I had come to love the Ragman. Every other face had faded in the wonder of this man, and I cherished him; but he died. I sobbed myself to sleep.

I did not know—how could I know?—that I slept through Friday night and Saturday and its night, too.

But then, on Sunday morning, I was wakened by a violence.

Light—pure, hard, demanding light—slammed against my sour face, and I blinked, and I looked, and I saw the last and the first wonder of all. There was the Ragman, folding the blanket most carefully, a scar on his forehead, but alive! And, besides that, healthy! There was no sign of sorrow nor of age, and all the rags that he had gathered shined for cleanliness.

Well, then I lowered my head and, trembling for all that I had seen, I myself walked up to the Ragman. I told him my name with shame, for I was a sorry figure next to him. Then I took off all my clothes in that place, and I said to him with dear yearning in my voice: "Dress me."

He dressed me. My Lord, he put new rags on me, and I am a wonder beside him. The Ragman, the Ragman, the Christ!

Donny, as if led by a force he did not quite understand yet, often ran out ahead of everyone. I would learn that he did so because his steps danced to a different tune and often it was the Lord Jesus Himself playing the music. What blind amazing faith.

With children, with grief, with life…please give those around you the space and privilege of being themselves, even if—especially if—it makes you uncomfortable.

One time when this child was three years old, I was filling up the car at the fuel station. He got out of his car seat (yes, he figured out how to do that, much to my dismay), ran to a car on the other side of ours, and started yelling at a man who was yelling at his child. Donny told him, "Stop doing that! He is a good boy." As the child in the back seat was weeping, Donny was pounding on the door trying to get in to comfort the child. I heard him calling, "Mama, help." I was already standing behind him.

I picked my boy up and walked over to the man, who was weeping also now. He hugged Donny and thanked him. Donny was allowed to hug the child who was being yelled at, and all was well in the world as we drove off.

When I asked this bear cub what made him do that, he said, "I could see Jesus over there trying to help, and I wanted to be with Him. Everything is always okay when you are with Jesus, Mama, and besides, I was only just standing behind Him." What a wonder. Always a wonder.

A conversation with Donny when he was in kindergarten (after a brief interlude with a teacher who had evolution on her mind) went like this: "What's the big deal about evolution, anyway? Don't those people know that even if we *did* come from monkeys, God made the monkeys, so they are still dumb for not believing in God! Besides, if we came from monkeys, why do we still have monkeys?" I will never forget walking down that school hallway with the boy whose thoughts were always bigger than his body!

Oh, the splendor of eyes that are open to beautiful things.

> "Settle down and see which ideas are good ideas and which are God's ideas. Preconception owns perception."
> –Donny Querin

## CHAPTER FOUR

# Donald Glen—
# The Silent Partner

"Pain and trial do not cause you to be something new; they cause you to be who you really are. Since identity is found where you spend your time, be sure to spend your time well… you will need a quality of time in your bones someday."

–Donny Querin

My father, Donald Glen Hardister, is the one whom my boy was named after. He would call Donny his "namesake." I want to tell you a bit about this one who purposefully poured into my boy from the day he was born. He is one of the most dynamic people you will ever meet. Today, at ninety-two years old, he is still thriving.

Dad tells stories of when he was very young calling out to Jesus. He was deathly ill, lying in his "little bed" at five years old, when he prayed and asked the Lord to heal him. He said the air became silent, and he was healed.

He learned that *faith is simply trusting Jesus to be Jesus and stepping away to allow the Holy Spirit to accomplish His will.* He would learn this truth over and over in his lifetime and model it as he went.

Two years later, he was very sick again. He asked his mother to pray, and she backed away from him and said, "Donald, you are almost a man [he was seven years old], pray for yourself. Build your faith!" She had an incredible gift of healing, but she would never speak of it.

When she heard him struggling in prayer, she told his brothers and sisters to go in and pray for him, then walked over and sat down on his bed. She never said a word. She simply offered her strong arm to him.

He wrapped his arms around hers, and again the air stood silent as he felt healing virtue come out of her arm into his. He was healed.

Throughout his life when he had a "promise to be fulfilled from God, coming or not," he remembered that God was good, even if he was bad. He said he would always pray that the Lord would make him a good boy, but then he ran into free will.

Dad rarely attended school because he was working and "organizing his neighborhood." He couldn't read or do academics perfectly, but God gave him a gift of architecture, mathematics and design. He has "street smarts" and a spiritual discernment that I have never seen matched.

He joined the local boxing club and became the Golden Gloves boxing champion in his region. He was also an apprentice carpenter who was paid eighty-eight cents per hour to practice "pounding nails" when he was just a boy. He would eventually become a journeyman carpenter and gifted home designer.

He taught Donny to be up before the birds and to work hard like Jesus is your boss. No complaining; just pulling and pushing. (See Philippians 2:14; Colossians 3:23–25; and 1 Timothy 5:8.)

One time Dad lifted the back end of a car up, and Donny asked him how he could do all these seemingly supernatural physical things. "If I need to be strong, then God will make me strong," he said. (See Psalm 18:34.)

He taught Donny that the Word of God was not an idea, but was always, always a fact. Even though he couldn't read, the Word of God was always precious to him. Donny would sit and read Proverbs and Psalms to his grandfather from the moment he knew how. Donny's philosophy from Psalm 18 would be modeled for a quarter of a century, and it mattered, right up to the end.

Dad taught Donny to live his life louder than the words he would speak. Louder than the hopes and disappointments he would have. Louder than those who would try to stop him. Louder than the pain he would have. Louder than the opinions of others. He would speak loudly with his life these words: "In spite of your trial and in spite of your pain, elevate another above yourself and, in so doing, you have elevated Jesus. Keep your mouth shut most of the time."

As a young man, while working as a volunteer fireman, Dad was run over by a fire truck while saving another man's life. His back would hurt him forever after that, and he would develop very painful arthritis and disc compression, among other things, in his spine and neck. There was no medication that would touch the pain. However, pain doesn't stop a champion.

Dad knew about pain, and so he taught my boy how to persevere through it. He taught all of us that. After suffering from this pain for well over sixty years, while he was watching a gospel singing show on the television, he said an angel walked into the room and instantly his back and neck were healed. No more pain.

The angel had giant feet and reminded him of the "angel" with giant feet that often came to visit his mother when he was a boy. She would always buy size 15 shoes for him whenever the thrift store had them available.

At almost every major life event, this "man," whom nobody knew, showed up, performing a needed miracle and giving advice. He wore the same clothes for decades, never aging, just changing his shoes from time to time. I guess they wear out!

He was there when two of Dad's brothers and his sister died and was a great comfort. He was there as the uninvited guest when his brother got married. He was there to give advice on how to fix a car when the five brothers were playing at shadetree mechanics. He was there during the midnight watch at Donny's bedside as I looked on in utter amazement. He was there when my grandmother was in an accident and left for dead. I tell you what, if this stuff wasn't just absolutely normal, it would be weird.

When my Donny was eighteen months old, he fell back and hit his head hard, very hard. He had a seizure, and I thought he passed out, but he had died. Calling 911 never entered my mind. My thoughts ran to Jesus.

I had my little Cynthia on my hip, so I put her in her playpen with her toys and picked Donny up, thinking I would wake him. He was cold and limp. He was not breathing.

I called my parents, and all I could do was scream on the phone with no words. Then I hung up. My dad was twenty minutes away, and he was at my house in ten minutes.

My cousin Ronnie, who was having a crisis of faith, was there with my dad. My dad told him to get in the car, and they drove like the wind. Ronnie told me later that my dad was begging God for Donny's life all the way to my house. He told Ronnie that the Lord showed him that his namesake had died.

My parents raised Ronnie and his brother Ricky as their own, and Ronnie said he had never seen my dad act that way before. He was completely weak in the hands of God, and we find that therein lies the source of our great strength. *Our strength is directly determined by the amount of our weakness that we have given over to God* (see 2 Corinthians 2:9–10).

I laid Donny on the couch and was weeping over him, rehearsing the story of the Shunammite woman and her son in my heart (2 Kings 4). I had forgotten to unlock the front door for the help I hoped was coming. Then, out of nowhere, came a bull in the fine china shop of my life. Dad had reared back and kicked my entire front door in. The doorjamb, hinges and trim went sailing across the entryway with the door.

He came over and grabbed my son, lifted him above his head, and marched him around the room. I can still see Donny's limp little body, lifeless, hanging like a worn-out rag doll on either side of my dad's massive hands.

Dad was in the Spirit if a man ever was. He was talking to Jesus in a language I did not understand. He was giving honor to God, and then he said, "Lord, You told me that my namesake would live…."

Then Dad laid my boy back down on the couch…and the air stood silent, again. We waited. Donny opened his eyes and said, "Oh, hi, Mama. I have been playing with Jesus in the river. The water is very crispy, and Jesus is very fun."

I fainted. I awakened in my dad's arms with Ronnie hugging Donny and crying. Donny was trying to console Ronnie with his big words (he began to speak at thirteen months old). Ronnie just kept crying and saying, "Jesus is real. He is real. I never saw anything like this. I never heard of anything like this before." Crisis of faith over.

My dad looked at me and said, "You did good. Always be account-able to your spiritual foundation. The Holy Spirit has trained you for this day, and you did not ignore Him." These were the lessons he would give over and over in so many ways as he has always been intimately partnered with the Holy Spirit over each life that he encounters.

My Donny would speak of this event until the day he went on ahead of us all into glory more than a quarter of a century later. He remem-bered the "crispy water"; he remembered how things smelled and felt. He remembered the expression on the face of Jesus. And he remem-bered how the air stood silent as Jesus told him he needed to go back to his house. He remembered his Grandpa. He remembered his destiny. He always remembered.

My husband insisted on a doctor's report to be sure Donny was fine, so we took him to the pediatrician that week. We were told that he was in perfect health, and, they said, "By the way, you were quite lucky because look at this cut on the base of his skull." (It had already begun to heal over by then as a secondary miracle.) "It is right in a spot that could instantly kill a child. This kind of traumatic brain injury can sev-er the brain stem and cause death." He looked at me and scolded me to be more careful. Donny!

Donny was literally only sick twice before leukemia came to get him. Once he had an ear infection that had enough sense to leave in a hurry after prayer. The other time, when he was six years old, he was vomiting with an uncontrollable fever. Donny shouted, "Get Grandpa!" So, I did.

My dad kneeled down next to Donny, put his giant hand on his grandson's very tiny forehead at the toilet, and embraced him there. He did not speak a word, but, somehow, I could hear him pray.

Big Don told little Don, "The devil doesn't have to go if you don't tell him to." So Donny told the devil to get off of him, and then he began to cry and thank Jesus for being his friend as my dad kneeled silently beside him with the rare tear streaming down his face. That day Donny was made well.

The fiber of Donny came from his Grandpa Don. Our children are cut from our souls, and it is beautiful. My boy, though, held real estate in my dad's soul.

When Donny knew he was not long for this earth, it was with Grandma and Grandpa that he held audience, alone, and none of them would speak of it. They had their goodbye long before he left, as if the grandson needed permission from the silent partner to go on ahead.

My father told me recently what they talked about. Donny wasn't sure if he could go, if he could be happy about going, and he felt he was going to go. Dad told him to remember that he came from a long line of people who know how to get up and push through whatever they are facing. "Your great-grandparents did, your grandma and I and your Mother have all had pain and sorrow, but we still get up and keep going. That is how you get rid of pain and sorrow and find comfort and joy; you have to get up, and you have to be thankful. No matter what God wants, you have to march into it."

After the three of them had that conversation years ago, I remember my Donny having a resolve and a joy that had, before then, tried to escape him from time to time. but, never again after that.

"Being Don" seems to be a lost art form. I can still hear this massive man speaking to a five-year-old boy as we walked across streams and meadows up near the Feather River in California. He would say, "You are going to do what you were born to do, no matter what." "No matter what" would come calling in a couple of decades. It was as if Dad knew that he needed to pour into this one, for his time was short. Dad always knew.

Of money, time and faith, Dad would say, "Give it away like you have it, or you will never have it." This saying has been his great philosophy of life, and he has applied the principle to every avenue he dared to walk down. Growing up, it was never a suggested path, but it was one he insisted on.

Once when my manchild was in the second grade, I was called into the principal's office because Donny and his little friends decided to "rearrange the playground" at school with destructive force.

My husband, his dad, was gone a lot, so I leaned on my dad, brothers and cousins for the father's influence over my son many times. They came with compulsion to put Donny through the paces of "why on earth have you done this"? They gave him the "don't be an idiot; birds of a feather fly together, so don't fly with dumb birds" speech. Not surprisingly, my boy would choose his friends wisely for the rest of his life.

Later when Donny was too sick to move and I needed him to take a shower while we were at University of California San Francisco (UCSF) medical center because the graft-versus-host disease from the bone marrow transplant was trying to take his skin, he would say, "Get Grandpa." Dad came and brought the "brothers" with him. He said, "Sometimes God brings a Volkswagen; today, He brought a Mack truck. Get up, boy!"

It is extravagant faith. It makes you wait; it makes you walk past hope and arrive at knowing. Even belief becomes weak in that land; it is compelled and even forced to become something greater: a reach toward perfect surrender and trust that sits in the middle of a yielding. They say discernment is a gift, but the grandson got it from the grandfather through watching and being willing to learn to discern.

My grandmother was in the hospital for three years after a car speeding at seventy-five miles per hour hit her and dragged her two hundred feet while she was exiting a bus in San Francisco. Most of her bones were broken. In fact, the doctor said all her bones were broken and they would never be able to set all of them. The family was told that she would never walk again. Furthermore, she was told that the nerve damage would plague her all her days with unbearable pain.

For two years after she was released from the hospital, she refused to stay down. She would roll the wheelchair off the back porch. She refused to stay in it. She would cut her casts off and haul herself where she needed to go with her legs lifelessly dragging behind her, leaving a bloody trail as she cited her conviction: "*The Lord will meet me where I am willing to drag myself.*"

Much to the dismay of the doctors and her family, she would not relent in her cause and conviction that God told her in her heart she would walk again. I never saw her as a cripple. She always walked and, in fact, marched.

The Great Reformer, Martin Luther, is often attributed with saying, "Prayer is not overcoming God's reluctance, but laying hold of His Willingness."

When my children were babies, Donald Glen would often stop by to see Donald Angelo and his baby sister Cynthia in the mornings before he went to work in the Sonoma countryside while the sun was still asleep. He would whisper a hope, to ask a favor of his God over them, and, yes, to sit still until the air became silent.

During those last days of his life on earth, Donny would say, "The devil is not in this sickness, Ma. You have to let me go; don't fight. Either God will keep me here or take me there. Grandpa, Grandma and I agree." And so peace abounds. Peace doesn't rest on what we want, but on what God wants.

I have never heard my dad read, but I have heard him pray.

> "Desire is tested by pursuit....Our daily task should be to challenge our limitations and prove the Lord's power beyond our weakest point. How haughty to even think we could reach our own human end. Without having experienced Christ's life, we are simply a whispering whine on a windswept canvas."
>
> –Donny Querin

## CHAPTER FIVE

# *Ministering Angels*

"You never know the trouble someone else is having, so you shouldn't be so prideful to think yours is special. We are each special; our troubles and trials, however, are not! Our daily task should be to challenge our limitations and prove the Lord's power beyond our weakest point. How haughty to even think we could reach our own human end. Without having experienced Christ's life, we are simply a whispering whine on a windswept canvas."

–Donny Querin

If you are still and listen very carefully, you will hear the footsteps of Jesus as He enters the room. He comes with a strong embrace—and the trouble leaves, for there is no darkness that can remain in His glorious light.

I had been sleeping on the couch in the living room next to my son who was in a hospital bed when a sound awakened me—a piercing sound. When sickness comes like a bullet, as it did for us, there are many sounds in the night. Sleep is far from you. But on this night, I slept until I did not.

*Behold, I send an Angel before you to keep you in the way and to bring you into the place which I have prepared* (Exodus 23:20 NLT).

It was 2:00 a.m. on January 19, 2009, when they came. Donny had been sick with leukemia and specifically the effects of the graft versus host disease due to the bone marrow transplant for over three years.

My beautiful boy had been beyond ill for three days. He had a nosebleed for thirty-six hours that would not stop, and it was profuse. He had a fever and was vomiting. He had not been able to eat much for almost a week. He had nothing for three days, yet the vomiting continued. His skin was very pale and very, very cold. The doctors and the home care nurse all recommended the ER. But we were not settled with that idea and had no peace in it. So, we waited. Just after 1:30 a.m., Donny finally nodded off to sleep. I went to the couch and watched him for a while, then I fell asleep.

I was awakened just moments later by a piercing sound, a noise I cannot quite put into words. It was a different kind of noise coming from the end of the hallway of the house.

It was a sound of keys rattling, of quiet whispers and doors closing. It was the sound of intention and compassion—heartfelt directives burdening the air with sound. You could feel perfect union coming down the hallway.

Then it happened. My vision opened up, and I saw five angels. Four were warriors with gold chain belts and keys on the belts. One was a worshipper. They had boots that went up to the knees. They were each dressed in different colors, but their clothes were trimmed in gold. They looked the same, except they had different trim or accents. The colors on the clothing were different, but the "style" was the same. All except for that worshipping angel—he looked different than the rest.

The warriors looked military somehow. Their garments seemed to be living, breathing things. I sat, my gaze transfixed upon them. They came in strong and determined. They were on a mission. The worshipping angel had his eyes on Donny the whole time. Even while walking down the hallway, his eyes were transfixed on Donny through the walls. He was very focused. The warring angels were on guard as they marched forward. They were looking at my boy, but at everything else also. They were completely on task and undistracted. The focus was incredible.

It put me in mind of a month or so ago when the family all gathered in Donny's hospital room at UCSF and "end it." A force came from heaven that day, and we knew that the Lord had come in all His power and ended the war over Donny's life. We knew he would be okay one way or the other, for we knew, like never before, that he was in the hands of the Almighty. I do not know why Donny was not miraculously healed with a powerful manifestation that day at UCSF, but God does what is best for His kingdom, and, as saints, we must be grateful for that. Walking out our trials with peace while the victory comes—however it comes—is a God-given right that we should not waste.

But, this week, something was wrong. Something "illegal" was going on in the spirit world, and we were helpless against it without divine intervention. Everything was uncontrollable and horrible.

They came to the end of the hallway, looked at me and then looked at Donny. The worshipping angel was immediately standing at the end of Donny's bed, leaning forward over Donny. This was his constant position throughout their stay. Then, and only then, another angel showed himself over the head of Donny's bed.

That was the same angel that had appeared when Donny was first admitted to the hospital three years earlier. It is the same one that appeared (I am sure accidently revealed!) when a car almost hit Donny when he was twelve years old. Donny "jumped" five feet in the air and was laid down softly in nearby grass as I looked on in complete awe. I then understood this to be his guardian angel. I guess they never leave, and this one needed a bit of help (I can't blame him), so they came!

This angel was in charge of my boy. That was clearly understood. It was clear to me that this angel came with my son at the moment of his birth—his guardian angel given by our precious Savior, Jesus. (See Psalm 91:11–12; Matthew 18:10; and Hebrews 1:14; 13:2.)

We do not worship angels (see Colossians 2:18), but from time to time some of us are given the privilege to see beyond the veil. It's not to interact, as some would say, but to see, to know and to be comforted.

In the moments that followed, I realized how foolish some people are who give angels instructions, have great conversations of direction with their angels, and command them this side of heaven. I don't think they are speaking to angels at all, but rather to the deceiver dressed up as an angel of light (see 2 Corinthians 11:14). Believe me, it is true.

Evidently, this guardian angel was there all along. Larger than the visiting worshipping angel that stood at the end of the bed. He stood with authority, an absolute majestic authority that was tangible. He was dressed in red, white and tan. The tan seemed to be opalescent and shimmered; light shifted from it and through it. He had wings that would ruffle now and again. He seemed to be uncomfortable that I was looking at him. I think he did not approve that he was seen!

He would gaze around for just seconds and then look back down on my boy. The tenderness and compassion that he had toward Donny made me question my own goodness and compassion. It truly was the most beautiful thing I had ever seen.

These angels were here to comfort and help, not commune—that is a privilege afforded to our Lord Jesus. He is the One who paid the price; He is the One with whom we commune. It was clear that these angels were not putting up with any foolishness and were not on a mission to have a conversation with a mere mortal. It was a trembling, magnificent, horrifying experience to see them; one should never be casual about such things.

The others surveyed the land, so to speak, then strategically placed themselves around Donny's bed. Four stood along the side of the bed that faced the backyard, so their backs were toward the yard and their faces singularly on Donny. The fifth stood watch at the end of the bed. The fifth never moved; he simply hovered over my boy.

They were all facing Donny and gently speaking to one another off and on as I sat and watched, helpless to even move. Breathing seemed like a full-time job at that point.

Just then the tallest and broadest of the warrior angels, the one in green, turned around and looked at me. He said, "Stay where you are." Then he pointed to the backyard and spoke to an entity lying in wait: "Be still. You have no power to prevail, and you will not call for any help." Just then a cage came from heaven and shut down upon the creature that was in the backyard, spiritually speaking. He coiled up and couldn't move or speak.

I turned back around to check on Donny, and they continued over him in such perfect care and concern. They were ministering to every single part of his body. They were touching him and feeding him. It looked like bread, but I couldn't tell and was not about to ask. He lay there, still, and would smile once in a while. He was sound asleep. At one point, he said, "Okay, angel. Thank you, okay, angel," still completely asleep. They were moving independently and yet in perfect unison.

When Donny went to sleep, he was ice cold. I had been massaging him for almost five hours, trying to warm him up and bring the tension out of his poor body. I wrapped him in warming blankets, and he went to sleep. I could see a part of his face between two of the angels standing around him, and it was red, beet red, as they were there with him. They were touching his eyes and ears and laying their hands on his stomach, chest and legs.

One angel began to collapse a bit as he touched Donny's hands and said, "Oh, to the great glory of God!" I couldn't hear much of what they said, but *that* I heard. They were giving me more time—more time with my boy—and he was willing to endure the pain to afford me, all of us, that.

The angels were moving about upon him and seemed very content. They were dressed in deep hunter green, aqua blue, a type of an orange color, or maybe it was rust, a white that had many layers along with different shades, and this profound-looking steel gray. My descriptions are horrible compared to what I saw. It has been engraved on my memory all these years. I had never seen colors like these before. The colors themselves were alive!

Their robes and sashes had a vast variety of trim of different shades of their main color. There were colors within colors and layers upon layers—the robes moved with a breeze that seemed to come from within them and around them. Splits in the robes revealed hidden weapons and these incredible boots and strength...such strength. They were beautiful to watch and peaceful to be around. Yet, somehow, there was a power, even a danger, to them that was comforting! The one dressed in green was the largest and did the talking if there were words that needed to be spoken.

He never asked a question, and I feel that if I had spoken, I would have been in some trouble. They each seemed to have their jobs, but I was not sure of what those jobs were. The worshipping angel at the end of the bed was all in white, with royal blue and purple trim. He held the same chain and keys as the others did. The worshipping angel was different in that he never moved, and his wings came out to cover Donny like a canopy from his feet up, joining in with the guardian angel, who covered him from the head down. He never took his gaze off of Donny, not even for a moment. The others did not show their wings. If they had any, I don't know.

The keys that they carried all had jewels on them. The angels that were dressed in orange/rust and green had medallions around their necks. They looked like medals or something. I never did find out what they were. Everything about the warrior angels were military and purposeful. They were strategic and tactical.

They stood and fed Donny and touched him for two hours. Then, the warring angels stood back, then moved forward toward Donny. They did this maybe five times. Moving backwards a few feet, then coming toward him in unison very slowly. I didn't know if they were building a hedge or barrier around him or just "checking their work," but what they were doing was very calculated and important.

It seemed like the worshipping angel was playing the role of protector during this time. He got more intense when the warrior angels moved back and forth than he had been before. Then the angels looked at each other, nodded and smiled. They looked at me and did the same. Then the angels looked at one another and stared at each other, including the guardian angel. This was the only time that angel really took his gaze off of Donny. The guardian angel looked up at the other angels, nodded his head and said to them, "Farewell, my brothers."

Then the warrior angels backed up again, away from Donny, walking backwards very slowly, checking on their "work" and being very careful to glance over his body with great intensity before they moved away. They turned and walked past me and went outside.

The worshipping angel stayed put and began to hover closer over Donny and held the arm of the guardian angel. I cannot be sure, but it seemed to me that the guardian angel had a tear in his eye. They both stayed there and didn't move. I looked out to the backyard to see what would happen, and I could see the ground open up. I saw smoke and flames and knew that it was a portion of hell showing itself. The warring angels each took a turn at fighting the demon.

It really wasn't much of a fight; they were slowly killing the demon and doing so with much punishment. It was almost like they were giving it what it had "earned" somehow. They commanded hell to watch, and then they beat the living daylights out of that thing. It was very evident that it did not take four of these warring angels to destroy this demon. It could have been destroyed at the sight of one of these angels.

The demon was captured and held there so they could almost make "sport" of it in front of hell. There was a message being sent that day. I remember Donny saying earlier, "Mom, it's as if all these complications have come from the enemy in an attempt to blaspheme God. The devil can't do that. However I am healed, it doesn't matter; the devil can't blaspheme God over my life by getting things messed up and trying to make me depressed. I need to do this right." If my life will have more impact by God taking me home, then that is what needs to happen, for His glory and testimony. And if I stay, I will not look back on this time as apparent weakness."

This demon cried and whimpered and then lay lifeless. The one in green threw the demon into the pit and the one in rust shouted, "You have no power to prevail over this one; do not return." The one in blue raised his hands over the hole and said, "To God alone is all praise and glory given."

Then the one in steel gray slowly walked forward. He moved his hands from each direction possible and said, "I place the seal of God Almighty here. From the north, the south, the east and the west." A waxy-looking substance appeared and sealed the ground, and he stomped it with his foot. He then looked up to heaven and raised his hands. The worshiping angel in white was out back now as well. They all stood on top of this seal and shouted, "Glory to God!"

The earth shook. Pictures on the walls in the house were physically sliding around. Then they looked at me and smiled, and the one in green said, "It is done, forever done. Be at great peace and go forward." Then he waved his hand at me, arched backward and looked up. He shouted something to the Lord. It seemed to take all the breath out of him, but I couldn't understand what it was. It was a glorious statement of some sort, I'm sure.

The angels, who moments ago were in full war mode, were now rejoicing as this one in green was making a great proclamation of some kind. Then they all raised their hands and formed fists and looked upward to heaven. Like a mighty rocket, all five took off together at the same time, and, in an instant, they were gone. They left a flash in the sky for just five seconds…white and gold. Whether it was seen in the flesh or by anyone else, I can't say. But I will never look at jet streaks the same way again!

The early morning was still and silent. I turned to look at my son as I stood at the door to the backyard. I could still see the guardian angel. All I could do was weep. He reached over and kissed Donny on the top of his head. Then he touched Donny's left hand, clasped it with both of his, looked at me and tenderly said, "You have prevailed in prayer." He reached over (I don't know how he did this) as if I was standing next to him, and he kissed both my eyes, hugged me and said, "All is well, daughter."

He held both of my hands for just a moment, and then I was back on the couch looking at Donny with this angel over him. He repeated the statement, "You have prevailed in prayer." I understood that he wasn't talking about "me" but about all of those who had prayed and fasted and held on for Donny. We dared to believe that God always knew what He was doing. This angel was speaking about everyone who held on for this moment. It truly had nothing to do with me. It has taken an army to hold my boy. I just had the privilege of being the girl on the couch.

God never promised an outcome in this; He simply wanted worship through it, as we truly accept whatever would be. When God promises an outcome, we hold for it and believe, for it is a promise. But, when God simply says, "Worship and Trust me," then that is what you do.

The guardian angel spoke a blessing over the house and all who would come by this way. Then, in words that I could not understand, he began to shout and speak things that I could not make out, but somehow I knew they were the proclamations of good things ordained of my God. More peace than I could hold up under filled the room. Such a power came from the corner of the room as this angel stood there, declaring his truth. Then he smiled, so deeply and tenderly at my Donny, as one who has always been by his side and we, just today, got to see him…he smiled at Donny, let go of his left hand, touched his right hand and made a mark on it. I want to say the mark was a cross, but I cannot be sure; he made strokes on Donny's hand with his index finger, quite slowly and methodically, very carefully.

As he looked at Donny and gently stroked him, I thought to myself, *This is clearly the most tender moment that I have ever seen.* He somehow put a mark of destiny on my son. Whether he would fulfill it here on the earth or in heaven beyond, I could not say, but whatever was to happen and whatever these unknown words and sentiments that the angels were speaking meant, I knew that all would be well with my soul. My boy would rest in the arms of his faithful God for his good and for His glory.

Donny was first and last on the angels' minds as they came to the aid of the guardian angel whose heart was breaking over my boy. The angel looked up, and I had never seen hope with a face, but I did that day, and it was incredibly comforting. That guardian angel rejoiced and wept over my boy.

I don't know if angels pray, but it seemed that this one was. He seemed to be bringing a petition or a praise before God, and it mattered. The angel wept and remained. He faded to take residence in my memory, and I didn't see him again until the day when the Lord sent a delegation to come and get my boy. I did not know it then, but Donny was glory bound. These are unexplainable, entirely unthinkable, things, but there it was.

The house turned quiet. I was standing next to Donny's bed. His face was still red—very, very red. His whole body turned red, then pale again. This process went on for thirty minutes. He seemed to be reverberating or pulsing with this deep red color. His oxygen levels had been between eighty-three and eighty-seven percent, and now they were ninety-nine and one hundred percent.

I was reminded of A.W. Tozer's statement: "God only fills that which has been emptied of itself."[2]

---

2 A.W. Tozer, *The Crucified Life* (Christian Publications, Inc., 1953).

Donny woke up around 6:00 a.m., looked at me and said, "I feel great, and I'm hungry, Ma, really hungry." I asked him if he remembered what happened in his sleep. He said, "No, but something happened. I feel well. Weak, but well." I told him the angels came and they were feeding him. He smiled the same smile that he had a few hours earlier when the angels were feeding him in his sleep, and he said, "The bread of life." His nose stopped bleeding, never to bleed again. He had no fever, and he never vomited again. He got stronger and stronger. He had not been able to walk for months, but that day he walked.

I had not known this (Donny told me later), but during our prayer time before sleep, he quietly asked the Lord to send angels to help him and protect him. He was very concerned that his mental state would end up destroying his spiritual state, and he was tired of fighting. He was not one to suffer depression, but it was trying to rob him, and he knew that. He missed his life, and the struggle was becoming an occupation. How I miss those times of prayer with my son. He was honest, profound and strangely innocent til the end.

Three friends of mine who don't know each other and live in different states each had almost this same scene in a dream four hours from each other on the same night this visitation occurred. A fourth friend said that she saw the Lord's angels encamped around Donny feeding and dressing him in the early hours of the morning. Two of these friends sent me the scripture reference of 1 Kings 19:4–8, which tells of the time an angel had bread prepared on the coals for Elijah to strengthen him on his journey. What a comfort.

My father, Donald Glen, called and said he was up at midnight asking the Lord to send angels to minister to Donny because he was very disturbed at the incredible pain he was in.

The Lord will bring us the help we need, often in rare and unusual forms, right when we need it. We need to be watching and aware and "in the Spirit on the Lord's Day" to hear the trumpet (Revelation 1:10 NKJV).

This visit would sustain Donny for over a year. He grew in strength. He wrote Bible studies, visited, counseled and prayed with people to encourage and help them. He would tell me that he was so grateful to have this time. I wrote down so much of what he said during that time, and his words remain a great pleasure and treasure to me and many others. What a gift this trial was, but especially that last year.

Then, in the young hours of the morning in the next year, very suddenly, his time would be up. What a sorrow. What a destiny. What an honor. What a privilege.

> "The greatest blessing we can give the Lord is to trust Him, and then it will be in the end what we wanted from the beginning…to honor the Lord God Almighty. I am marked with a desire to first understand and increase my breadth of perspective through being willing for constant change. If you could control things, you would limit them, and, if you could contain them, you would constrict them."
>
> –Donny Querin

## CHAPTER SIX

# *Becoming a Citizen of Heaven*

"During our trials, the responsibility we have to the Lord is increased because people are watching very closely to learn how it's done. Bear your cross as a privilege, knowing that God Himself has made you strong enough to go through it and arrive on the other side of your adversity as a bright light for God's glory. Attitude is a decision. If I let myself lose sight of my testimony, I could get really depressed in the middle of this. Our trials should be examples to others of how to handle adversity. If we lean on God, *He* actually handles it for us. Every trial has a huge potential value for others to learn from as they watch you and attempt to glorify God; this is why we must never give up. Every situation is unique in what it allows us to learn. Allow it!"

–Donny Querin

Donny had said all along that, during his twenty-eighth year, something special was going to happen to him. He had known this since he was little. When he contracted leukemia, we all thought that meant he would be healed in his twenty-eighth year. The truth was, the Lord was trying to tell us that we only got him for twenty-eight years.

The day before he left (nine days before he turned twenty-nine), he said, "If the Lord was to take me, I just want to be sure that He'll be able

45

to tell me I did everything He told me to do. I don't expect Him to tell me I did it good, but I do want Him to know that I tried, and I want Him to know that I did my best."

I looked at him in silence, knowing the incredible pain he endured in an effort to honor his Savior. All I had was tears. When we both got emotional, one of us would either say, "Jesus wept" (John 11:35 NKJV) or "From henceforth let no man trouble me: for I bear in my body the marks of the Lord Jesus" (Galatians 6:17 KJV). "Henceforth" became our code word for, "hang in there, it will be worth it all." I tried to understand his pain but I knew he understood mine.

He said, "I just wanted everyone around me to get closer to God. I told the Lord when I first got sick, 'Whatever it takes to bring people closer to You, Lord. Whatever it takes.' I never minded my pain because I was being brought closer to the Lord, and I had the privilege of bringing people with me."

It was a beautiful conversation we had on his last day on earth. Such a lionhearted bear cub of a boy. "Whatever it takes" is apparently a heavy order.

His face lit up. He mustered all the strength he had to sit up straight in that ICU bed. He said, "Do you see that?"

"What?"

"You are kidding me! Surely you see that?"

"I don't...what?"

He told me with the excitement of a boy two decades younger, like the boy telling me about the crispy water and playing in the river with Jesus, "Those three angels dressed in gold standing like statues over there."

"Nope!"

He proceeded to tell me that they were of average to tall height. They stood, three together, in the corner of the room with their hands clasped in front of themselves. Waiting. For what, we didn't know. "Dressed in gold" seems like a party, so I was figuring they had come to bring him a miracle. I couldn't have been more wrong! Watch out for angels dressed in gold.

The guardian angel once again revealed himself at the head of Donny's bed, never far from his beautiful face. He was looking at Donny with such admiration and adoration. The guardian angel Donny did not see, but those others…wow!

I can only assume that the angels dressed in gold came to escort him to glory. I did not see them then, but when he passed on, I looked up and saw five gold flashes dart across the sky. They paused and then dashed upward and out of sight. Often, things are rarely as they seem. Three angels in gold, plus Donny and his guardian angel—this is a completely comforting truth.

As he lay on that hospital bed, beyond agony, Donny looked at me and said, "I'm done. I really think I'm done." He said, "You have been a good mother, and I love you very much. Thanks for getting me here. Tell Sister she is of my soul and my heart; tell Dad I love him; and tell my Amy…she is my favorite thing, my great blessing from the Lord. It has been an honor to love her."

I said, "Now, now, Donny," as one would do. I rubbed his feet for a couple of hours to try and help his horrible neuropathy before they came to intubate him. At that moment I saw those three angels dressed in gold, and I was disturbed. They walked down the hall behind the hospital bed as the guardian angel hovered over the bed above Donny's head.

Shortly thereafter the medical staff stuck a tube down his throat and found that his lungs were unable to carry the weight of life in him. The doctors did a beautiful job, but Donny's day was done, and his time was up. He spent an entire day struggling to breathe, and it was very, very painful for him. Just a couple of hours later…and my boy was gone. Glory bound.

I know that this is for the glory of God because Donny told me it was. What an amazing wonder that one could serve God through such pain. Life is full of memories, so spend them well.

We held hands around Donny's bed and embraced his broken frame. We rejoiced and thanked God that he had the privilege of coming and we had the privilege of knowing him. Each one of us shared our heart, shared our feelings together, as we could feel Donny already beginning his next call. We thanked the Lord with broken hearts. Each one of us had our alone time with Donny, and it was a very special time. I'm so grateful that the Lord afforded us this time. We knew he was out of pain and that he accomplished the purpose by which he came, but the sorrow that came with his moving on was almost unsurmountable.

As each of us took our time alone with Donny, I wanted to find my way to the chapel, as I would spend my alone time with him last.

Walking out of the ICU, slowly pushing through those big double doors, I saw three women standing there. They immediately rejoiced at seeing me. I did not know who they were, but they knew me. Evidently, I had spoken at their church up north, and they had been praying for someone to come and pray for their father who was dying in the ICU. Surely this was an incredible coincidence. I just wanted to be alone to grieve my great loss.

As these women pleaded with me to go pray for their father, this scripture came to my mind: "...Be instant in season, out of season" (2 Timothy 4:2 KJV). So, I went back into the ICU, as far as I could tell, incredibly "out of season." The women never knew that my son had died that very hour; there was no reason for them to know. This man's room was just two doors down from Donny's. That man rose up to live as my son lay lifeless. "Really, God? Really?"

God is just. However, we find justice and fairness often to be vastly and disturbingly different. Either way, we serve the One, and so, in spite of ourselves, it has just got to be okay. "How much of my heart does Jesus own?" is my constant question before myself as I hold the knife of obedience to my throat.

I eventually found my way to the chapel. I guess I have been in one chapel or another more times than not over the fourteen years since Donny's passing. I stopped trying to make sense of it; instead, I simply rejoice in it because my boy is happy and I trust my God. He, too, watched His precious Son, Jesus, suffer, and the world is better for it.

We cannot begin to ask God "why," for His ways are greater than ours, and we shall never understand so many things on this side of glory. But, trust...we can trust Him.

> *For my thoughts are not your thoughts, neither are your ways my ways, saith the Lord. For as the heavens are higher than the earth, so are my ways higher than your ways, and my thoughts than your thoughts* (Isaiah 55:8–9 KJV).

Grief is never the same for any two people. Donny went to the hospital many times, and he always came home. To lose him was unbelievable for all of us to wrap our minds around. However, we had the privilege of a long goodbye, and I am grateful.

> *Trust in the Lord with all thine heart; and lean not unto thine own understanding. In all they ways acknowledge him, and he shall direct thy paths* (Proverbs 3:5–6 KJV).

Throughout his journey, Donny had many miracles along the way. The hospital sent him home to die, and he lived three more years. What pain he endured, what triumph he achieved! It was a difficult path for us all, especially for him, but we are all grateful to be surrounded by those who joy in the journey.

Two nights after he left, I had a dream, which was incredibly vivid. I dreamed that Donny was swimming in the ocean with friends. He was surfing with whales. An angel came to the beach and motioned for him to come, and he did. The angel oddly reminded me of that guardian angel.

As he walked out of the water, his swimming trunks turned into royal robes, and the angel and Donny talked and laughed as they went to a large meeting hall, which was massive. Beautiful shiny wood was everywhere with large—very large—doors; they were incredibly tall and were rounded on top. Donny and the angel were there almost instantly. It looked like 10,000 angels were in attendance. Jesus stood on one side of the stage, and Donny came in from the other side; they smiled and waved. Jesus stood watch as Donny asked for questions.

One angel raised his hand and stood up. He said, "I have a question about helping people. They seem to have no hope and are not looking for help, and it appears that they don't even want help."

Donny answered in his Donny way. His personality and mannerisms were completely intact. I would think this was just me, having a dream about my boy, but a day later two friends who don't know each other and live in separate states told me of dreams they had the night before that were almost exactly the same as mine. Yet, they had never met my son.

Anyway, Donny said, "You have to seek to understand before you can expect to be understood. There is little hope on the earth, and people don't trust." Then Donny asked for examples of what the angel was talking about.

The angel responded, "For instance, I tried to help someone with her groceries who had small children. She was struggling. I wanted to put the bags in the vehicle for her. She said, 'No, thank you,' and hurried away. How do I fix that?"

Donny laughed his laugh and gave this explanation: "You have to let them know that you are from around there, that you are not a stranger to the store or the area, that you are going in to shop now. Let them know you have other things to do, so they know that you are not stalking them. Gently go, and they will receive the comfort you are mandated to bring."

A year passed after that dream, and I found the strength to go to the local large warehouse store. I had not been there in over five years, and it can be exhausting. This day was just as I remembered: exhausting. I had hurt my arm and forgot I would have to unload all these groceries.

I pulled the large cart up to the back of my SUV and just stood there, trying to figure out how to get this all done. I looked down and took a deep breath, and a man came up next to me literally out of nowhere. He had a leather vest on and was adorned with bright red, long curly hair and was wearing bell bottom jeans. He seemed a bit out of his decade.

He put his hand on the cart and started this conversation with me in the parking lot: "Hello there, you seem pretty wore out. I live right around the corner, and I come to this store all the time. In fact, I am going in now. But first, I would sure like to help you put these groceries away. Would that be okay?"

"Uh…huh." I stood staring.

I could not move. He put everything away for me. Then he took the cart and said he would return it. I stood there weeping in the parking lot. He stopped, turned around and said, "Thank you for letting me help you. And, your son is very proud of you." Then he was just *gone*.

*Be not forgetful to entertain strangers: for thereby some have entertained angels unawares* (Hebrews 13:2 KJV).

"Without a Trace"
by Donny Querin
May 3, 2007 (eight months into leukemia)

With open arms full of grace
and a passion-driven fire,
He took it all away—
my sin without a trace.
Someone had to pay the price;
a sinful nature seals our fate.
He is waiting for His Bride,
yet from the tree we still partake.
Take up your cross and run the race;
one day you will arrive with Him in Eternity,
And you will know that your sin is gone,
without a trace.

## CHAPTER SEVEN

# *Grief Beyond the Loss*

"Acceptance from the world creates a distance from God. When trials come, we can decide to crawl in a cave of depression, and, in so doing, we agree with the world and accept its pathetic standards, or we can pull the spiritual muscle from our foundation and soar for the glory of God.

"Stumbling through trials and tribulation never helped anyone, dead or alive. Trials produce the greatest exercise of Faith and Grace if they are handled properly. Walk through this trial with force because the cause for Eternity...a blood-stained cross, sits in your heart. Embrace the unexpected; it is no surprise to Jesus."

–Donny Querin

*Verily I have cleansed my heart in vain, and washed my hands in innocency* (Psalm 73:13 KJV).

David Wilkerson spoke about this psalm in his sermon, "Someone to Watch Over Me."

Asaph, the writer of this psalm, was so confused by his sufferings in comparison to the easy life of the wicked that he nearly slipped into a pit of absolute unbelief. He was ready to accuse God of abandoning him, of not being concerned, and for a moment he was ready to quit the battle and give up completely.

This godly man must have thought, "I've been doing right and enduring hardships all this time but it was for nothing. All my diligence, my praising and worshiping, my study of God's Word has been useless, in vain. I have done only right; yet I continue to suffer and it makes no sense. What's the use of going on?"[3]

David Wilkerson explains that we need to "guard" our hearts against "slipping," especially when we or a loved one is enduring a trial or dealing with grief. Like Asaph, we may wonder why God allows these things. Asaph went to the temple to pray and discovered that God had a plan. He realized that God was a loving Father to him, as He is to us. The sermon concludes:

Asaph began to see the whole picture and he rejoiced: "God is the strength of my heart, and my portion for ever" (verse 26). He could say, "Yes, my strength is failing. Yes, I'm enduring a great battle – but I'm not alone in my struggles. I have a loving Father in heaven and He watches over me!"[4]

When you are dealing with grief, it can come at you like a heat-seeking missile. You cannot avoid it, manage it or calm it down. It wants what it wants, when it wants it. It is best to yield to the Lord in the middle of it and deal with what you feel; otherwise, the grief will cause you to be "grief-stricken," and then, well, you are stuck for a very long and miserable time. Grief and change are inevitable, but misery and doubt are not. Misery and doubt are optional.

A month after Donny left, we attended GriefShare meetings, which were helpful in their own way for each of us. Grief has no rules, and, if it did, it is rude and would not follow them. A book I found invaluable was *The Grief Recovery Handbook* by John W. James and Russell Friedman (further resources are listed in the Appendix). It reminds us of the five stages of grief and death and that grief pays compound interest;

---

3 David Wilkerson, "Someone to Watch Over Me," SermonIndex.net, Copyright © 2022-2024, accessed August 13, 2024, https://www.sermonindex.net/modules/articles/index.php?view=article&aid=35690.
4 Ibid.

one grief or disappointment piles up on top of another and grows until it is dealt with. You deal with it, or it deals with you.

There are many kinds of grief. For some people, not being chosen in grade school for the baseball team brings grief; others could care less. Those who are shaken by these episodes of life make deposits of grief in their souls, and, if they don't deal with that grief, their next episode of disappointment is worsened. Then, when an actual horrible loss comes, they collapses under it. They become grief-stricken.

Please tend to disappointments and loss in yourself and those around you. Ignoring or punishing a child's disappointment, sadness and pain only teaches that child to grieve alone or not at all. If he or she is a naturally sensitive child, this will cause that child to be at odds with his or her identity and the beauty of how God made him or her. There is a wicked self-condemnation and guilt that lives where grief simmers. And, the worst part is that it is learned. Tears have great value; do not be afraid to acknowledge them. All things are useful for their time.

The following quote is attributed to the great author, Washington Irving, of two hundred years ago, "There is a sacredness in tears. They are not a mark of weakness, but of power. They speak more eloquently than ten thousand tongues. They are messengers of overwhelming grief, of deep contribution, and of unspeakable love."

Most people told me to "be careful" of that first year. So, I was very careful not to allow myself to be too reflective and, instead, to stay busy, surrounded by my champions of pain and faith.

Then, the second year hit, and what a train wreck that was! I didn't see it coming. I pushed through and accomplished my tasks and kept preaching and teaching and doing and being. But, it was difficult, very difficult, and then it became a little easier. I miss my boy every day, and you miss your loved one every day, and all the moments that make up a day. Understanding that you and I take them with us as we move forward is a considerable help. Never, ever, get over the loss; simply merge and evolve into the glory of what is the new normal. God has a purpose.

Something that will really help you is to not be sorrowful that your loved one is not here for certain events. "Donny *would have* loved this or done that...." These statements pull you into the depths of despair, and there is no real exit.

Instead, I remembered that he *was* there, in my heart, and looking on from heaven. It made going forward easier. You do not "get over" the one who has left;, you "go on" with him or her in your heart.

You may feel alone, but that is a lie. You are simply lonely for the one you lost, and the Lord has not left you. Donny used to say, "Abide with God in the stillness...He lives there and visits everywhere else!" This you can do. Tend to the garden of your heart because it is important, for you are important.

You will see your loved one again because the Bible says you will. In the meantime...

> *Fear thou not; for I am with thee: be not dismayed; for I am thy God: I will strengthen thee; yea, I will help thee; yea, I will uphold thee with the right hand of my righteousness* (Isaiah 41:10 KJV).

The renowned pastor and author A. W. Tozer said:

The neglected heart will soon be a heart overrun with worldly thoughts. The neglected life will soon find itself in moral chaos. The church that is not jealously protected by mighty intercession and sacrificial labors will before long become the abode of every evil bird and the hiding place for unsuspected corruption. The creeping wilderness will soon take over that church that trusts in its own strength and forgets to watch and pray.[5]

It takes time, but you will get there. As you and I lean on the Lord, we both get there. I wish for you goodness, joy, peace and patience as you pursue His great call upon your life. Things are not over for you; this is time to forge ahead.

To God be the glory, at all times and in all things. After all, if He is in charge of one thing, then He must be in charge of everything!

---

5 A. W. Tozer, *From the Grave: A 40-Day Lent Devotional* (Chicago: Moody Publishers, 2017), Day 1.

*O Lord, thou hast searched me, and known me. Thou knowest my downsitting and mine uprising, thou understandest my thought afar off. Thou compassest my path and my lying down, and art acquainted with all my ways. For there is not a word in my tongue, but, lo, O Lord, thou knowest it altogether. Thou hast beset me behind and before, and laid thine hand upon me. Such knowledge is too wonderful for me; it is high, I cannot attain unto it. Whither shall I go from thy spirit? or whither shall I flee from thy presence? If I ascend up into heaven, thou art there: if I make my bed in hell, behold, thou art there. If I take the wings of the morning, and dwell in the uttermost parts of the sea; even there shall thy hand lead me, and thy right hand shall hold me. If I say, Surely the darkness shall cover me; even the night shall be light about me. Yea, the darkness hideth not from thee; but the night shineth as the day: the darkness and the light are both alike to thee. For thou hast possessed my reins: thou hast covered me in my mother's womb. I will praise thee; for I am fearfully and wonderfully made: marvellous are thy works; and that my soul knoweth right well. My substance was not hid from thee, when I was made in secret, and curiously wrought in the lowest parts of the earth. Thine eyes did see my substance, yet being unperfect; and in thy book all my members were written, which in continuance were fashioned, when as yet there was none of them. How precious also are thy thoughts unto me, O God! how great is the sum of them! If I should count them, they are more in number than the sand: when I awake, I am still with thee* (Psalm 139:1–18 KJV).

As my friend Keith Carroll says, "Being thankful and grateful is the best healer of your soul. Allow your grief over missing them to become a praise and thanksgiving for them. We all are more effective by transforming our emotions of grief into expressions of praise. Spend time thanking God for their life and the privilege that you had in being an important part of their life."

And to that end, I give you Joseph, the wonder boy of the Old Testament.

As far as people who are given a rough life to live, Joseph is our guy. His mother died, and he was overprotected by his father and hated by his siblings. I think Joseph just had this incredibly innocent heart, for having dreams and sharing them with people who barely tolerated him, let alone celebrated him and anything the Almighty showed him, was not brilliant.

In Genesis 37 he starts with a hard time, being sold into slavery by his own siblings after kindly bringing food to them. One can only imagine all that went with that event. His crying out to be rescued was probably met with sneering laughter. And, remember, he was just a young man, a boy, really.

Nevertheless, he kept believing that God had a purpose for him. False accusations led to prison time. Those whom he helped, forgot about him and abandoned him. But he never gave up hope because he never quit thanking God. Rejection could not stick to him because his identity was in God and confirmed by his thankful heart.

Time passed and he was reconciled to his family. In Genesis 50:20 (NKJV) he says, "But as for you, you meant evil against me; but God meant it for good, in order to bring it about as it is this day, to save many people alive."

*He moved in a thankfulness that hinged on forgiveness and took a grateful heart to a new level.*

> *Enter into his gates with thanksgiving, and into his courts with praise: be thankful unto him, and bless his name.* (Psalm 100:4 KJV).

What an amazing miracle. What an amazing testimony. I love that the story of Joseph is in the Bible.

In the arms of thankfulness, we reach a deep gratefulness that covers all that ails us as a blanket and ushers us into worship where grief is minimized. We are made well there.

Thankfulness brings into our lives that extra reward the Bible talks about. The extra blessing. The added bonus. The thing that not everybody else gets. And even, surely, the blessing we were not even counting on. (See Psalm 103:2–5; Philippians 4:6–7; and James 1:2–4.)

Donny wrote this a year before he was laid to rest:

As quickly as the sun sets, the pages of our lives turn. We travel the world, each empty for something of substance. Our souls yearn. Pages turn to chapters; days turn to years. Hardships come and go, and with it…pain. But when we reach the end, we'll know our efforts were not in vain.

We make the most of every moment, knowing that it may be our last. We see each other grow and change, a true transformation from the past. Ah, to be vulnerable with someone—that is where the depth is, to see true care and concern only paralleled by His. True friendship, real friendship, transcends the laws of individuality. You find that, in the end, we are who we are because of the measure of Christ in us as we love each other.

Our time is coming to an end, and our paths will soon part. We will look back on the good and the bad and say, yes, you will always be in my heart. The memories we have together, one could never count or catalog. It would be like trying to measure the drops of dew in a heavy morning fog.

So, this is the day and time we've been given. Let us not put it to waste; for the hour is coming when we will disappear without notice. Someday people will read about us. They'll say you were my family, and I was your brother; they will read on and on and on. And they will find that all we have on this earth outside of Christ is each other.

Thank you for walking through my dear son's life here in these pages. It is my hope and prayer for you that you have been encouraged and enlightened. May you find joy, love and contentment in all that you do, holding every blessing that heaven can afford to place upon you while you tread upon this sod and soil.

*...We went through fire and through water: but thou broughtest us out into a wealthy place* (Psalm 66:12 KJV).

[Give] *thanks always for all things to God the Father in the name of our Lord Jesus Christ* (Ephesians 5:20 NKJV).

*And let the peace of God rule in your hearts, to which also you were called in one body; and be thankful* (Colossians 3:15 NKJV).

# *Appendix*

Included here are some books beyond the Bible that Donny read and studied from until he sailed on in 2010. All are not listed, but I thought you might enjoy some of these.

You can see by the titles how he was ever ready to prepare; his marriage was young, and he read many books on marriage before he ever met his dear Amy. (They married three months after his diagnosis.)

He was a business major and had started his own business before he was struck down. I have narrowed down his books on business to his favorites.

He left before he had children, but he read many books on parenting. He wanted to be ready in case he was able to have children. Sweet boy. Smart man.

This list is in no particular order.

*The Conquest of Canaan* by Jessie Penn-Lewis
*God's Generals* by Roberts Liardon
*A Shepherd Looks at Psalm 23* by W. Phillip Keller
*The Case for Christ* by Lee Strobel
*The Sacred Romance: Drawing Closer to the Heart of God* by Brent Curtis and John Eldredge
*Wild at Heart* by John Eldredge
*The Screwtape Letters* by C. S. Lewis
*A Grief Observed* by C. S. Lewis
*How People Grow: What the Bible Reveals About Personal Growth* by Henry Cloud and John Townsend
*The Circle of Innovation* by Tom Peters
*Making Love Last Forever* by Gary Smalley
*The Key to Your Child's Heart* by Gary Smalley
*Love Is a Decision* by Gary Smalley and John Trent
*If Only He Knew* by Gary Smalley
*The 21 Irrefutable Laws of Leadership* by John C. Maxwell

*Winning with People* by John C. Maxwell

*Developing the Leader Within You* by John C. Maxwell

*Developing the Leaders Around You* by John C. Maxwell

*The 17 Indisputable Laws of Teamwork* by John C. Maxwell

*Trickle-Down Morality: Returning to Truth in a World of Compromise* by Don S. Otis

*The One-Minute Manager* by Ken Blanchard and Spencer Johnson

*The Fear of the Lord* by John Bevere

*The Bait of Satan* by John Bevere

*A Heart Ablaze* by John Bevere

*The God Chasers* by Tommy Tenney

*A Commitment to Valor* by Rod Gragg

*As a Man Thinketh* by James Allen

*God's Armor Bearer* by Terry Nance

*Why You Act the Way You Do* by Tim LaHaye

*Dare to Discipline* by James C. Dobson

*The Strong-Willed Child* by James C. Dobson

(Interestingly enough, Donny read the books I used to help raise my children; in college, Donny carried my highlighted and faded copies with him—a treasure.)

*Why Revival Tarries* by Leonard Ravenhill

*Men Are from Mars, Women Are from Venus* by John Gray

*Pour Your Heart Into It* by Howard Schultz

*The Upside-Down Kingdom* by Donald B. Kraybill

*The Heart of Change* by John P. Kotter and Dan S. Cohen

*His Needs, Her Needs* by Willard F. Harley, Jr.

*No More Excuses* by Tony Evans

*Understanding the Purpose and Power of Woman* by Myles Munroe

*The 5 Love Languages* by Gary Chapman

*The Celebration of Discipline* by Richard J. Foster

*Pure Desire* by Ted Roberts

*Critical Mass* by Mario Murillo

*The Cost of Discipleship* by Dietrich Bonhoeffer

*The Prayer of Job* by Sandra Querin

*The Prayer of Moses* by Sandra Querin

*The 7 Habits of Highly Effective People* by Stephen R. Covey

*Cross-Cultural Conflict* by Duane Elmer
*Lincoln on Leadership* by Donald T. Phillips
*Shadow of the Almighty* by Elisabeth Elliot

For more help with your grief, please refer to *The Grief Recovery Handbook* by John W. James and Russell Friedman.

To follow our journey through leukemia, please go to www.DonnysJourney.com.

For instructions and helps on a revival lifestyle, go to www.TheRevivalCenter.info or www.abbasheart.com.

# About the Author

S andra Hardister Querin was called at the age of nine to "prepare for the day" when she would preach the Good News. Although hampered by cystic fibrosis and it's complications for thirty years, she pursued the call of God and her education, holding an MBA, JD, MDiv and ThD. She married her high school sweetheart and was married for forty-five years. Sandi worked as a college professor and corporate executive as well as serving on staff of several churches until the Lord called her into full-time ministry.

She has been supernaturally healed of her disease and walks in miraculous healing power. Her ministry encompasses the heart of Christ and is predominately prophetic. The cry of her heart is for the lost to be saved and for the saved to be empowered by Jesus Christ.

Sandi travels the world spreading the gospel and bringing hope to the hurting, healing to the broken, and deliverance to all those who embrace the cross of Christ. The sick come to her meetings for their miracles and are not disappointed because Jesus does not disappoint. Sandi serves as a leader at The Revival Center in Clovis, California. To follow the services online or to find out more about Sandi and her ministry, go to www.abbasheart.com.

She enjoys her children, grandchildren, the many adventures her friends take her on when she is not traveling and serves as a Fresno County chaplain.

*The Prayer of Donny* is the third book in the "Honest to God" series, following *The Prayer of Job* and *The Prayer of Moses*.

To reach Sandi, write or call:
1516 Draper Street
Kingsburg, CA 93631
559.897.9575

Or view her YouTube channel: The Revival Center, Clovis, California.